Comprehensive formulas for the CFA® Level I Exam

SECOND EDITION

EMMANUEL ALUKO, CFA

Baseline Educational Services

ISBN-13: 978-1492794356

ISBN-10: 149279435X

ISBN-13 : 978-1492794356

ISBN-10 : 149279435X

About the Author

Emmanuel Aluko, CFA, MBA, MS, BSc, IMC

Emmanuel Aluko is an engineer, businessman and educator. He is currently the director of Baseline Educational Services Limited, a training firm based in London focussed on financial and business education.

He worked for six years for Schlumberger Oilfield Services as an engineer from 1992 to 1998, training in the United Kingdom and working in Nigeria and India. He has a first class degree in Mechanical Engineering from the Obafemi Awolowo University in Nigeria (1992), a Master of Science degree in Petroleum Engineering from the University of Texas at Austin (2000), and a Masters in Business Administration (MBA) degree from the London Business School (2002). He completed the Investment Management Certificate (IMC) from the CFA Society of the UK in 2002. He took the CFA level III exam in June 2009 and was granted the CFA charter in 2009. Emmanuel is a regular member of the CFA Institute and the CFA Society of the UK (CFA UK) since July of 2009.

Dedicated to my wife Roz

Contents

Preface to the second edition

This is a compilation of formulas, specifically addressed to the CFA® Level I exam, the first exam in a series of three exams en-route to the completing the CFA® program and eligibility for the CFA® Charter upon meeting work experience requirements and standards of professional conduct. The CFA® Program is a highly respected educational program that stresses the highest standards of integrity, education and professional excellence.

The book is intended to be used as a supplement to the CFA® curriculum. It contains no examples, as those are well covered in the CFA® curriculum and including examples will result in a duplication of effort. The book is a reference book with application across the body of financial knowledge, reflecting the breadth of the CFA® Program at level 1. Thus, finance students and professionals across the board will find it useful.

Any errors in the book are mine. In the second edition, technical analysis formulas have been added and a reformatting of all the formulas was undertaken. Efforts have been made to review all the formulas for accuracy. Some of the symbols are different from those in the curriculum and this has been done to employ alternative usage common in the teaching of finance, an example of which is using the letter "r" for cost of capital, rather than "k". Some formulas appear multiple times, with slightly different notation in order to address the curriculum section. Some formulas have been inferred from the reading, and may not be noticeable in the readings as examples may have been used to illustrate the formula. In addition, this work is not complete, as no work ever is. However, it is comprehensive as per the curriculum.

Any suggestions for improvement or errors that users may find in the book can be sent to tuition@baselineeducation.co.uk. If you are in the CFA® Program at level I, I wish you all the best. If you are not in the program, the program is worth considering for the benefits it brings. You can explore the CFA® Program at https://www.cfainstitute.org/cfaprog/. For me, the CFA® Program was an enjoyable learning experience, obviously without the exams. I hope this book makes the exams a lot easier.

Acknowledgments

This book is a result of standing on the shoulder of giants, those who have educated me from my early years, to those who are still educating me now. Rather than list names, I list schools or institutions that I have encountered in the course of my ongoing educational experience:

1. Staff School, University of Ife (Now Obafemi Awolowo University), Ile-Ife, Nigeria.
2. Staff School, University of Benin, Benin City, Nigeria.
3. Federal Government College, Ido-Ani, Nigeria.
4. The Obafemi Awolowo University, Ile-Ife, Nigeria.
5. The Schlumberger British Training Centre, Livingston, Scotland.
6. The University of Texas at Austin, Department of Petroleum and Geosystems Engineering, Austin, Texas, USA.
7. The London Business School, London, England.
8. CFA Society of the UK, London, England.
9. The Institute of Financial Services, London, England.
10. The CFA Institute, Charlottesville, Virginia, USA.

My thanks to all those who have been generous enough to employ me or pay me for my services. My special thanks to my parents for giving me the grounding for who I am, and my wife, Roz, for coping with me.

Emmanuel Aluko
Baseline Educational Services Limited
London
November 2013.

1. Quantitative Methods

Time value of Money and Discounted Cash Flow applications

1. Market interest rate, r

$$r = r_f + i + r_d + r_l + r_m$$

Where:

r_f – real risk free rate of interest
i – Inflation premium
r_d – default risk premium
r_l – liquidity premium
r_m – maturity premium

2. Present Value and Future Value (Discrete compounding)

$$PV = \frac{FV}{\left(1 + \frac{r_a}{m}\right)^{mn}} \qquad ; \qquad FV = PV\left(1 + \frac{r_a}{m}\right)^{mn}$$

Where:

PV – Present value
FV – Future value
r_a – annualised rate of interest
m – Number of compounding periods per year
n – Number of years

3. Present Value and Future Value (Continuous compounding)

$$FV = PV * e^{rt} \qquad ; \qquad PV = FV * e^{-rt}$$

Where:

FV – Future Value
PV – Present Value
e - Euler number or Napier Number that is equal to 2.71828183 to 8 decimal places and is also the base of the natural logarithm
r – Annual interest rate
t- Time in years

4. *Effective, periodic and annual interest rates (discrete compounding)*

$$r_p = r / m \quad ; \quad EAR = (1+r_p)^m - 1$$

5. *Effective and annual interest rates (continuous compounding)*

$$EAR = e^r - 1$$

Where:

r_p – periodic interest rate
r – Annual rate
m – Number of compounding periods
EAR – Effective annual rat e

6. *Present Value and Future Value of an Annuity (ordinary annuity)*

$$PV_A = \frac{A}{r_p}\left(1 - \frac{1}{\left(1 + r_p\right)^{mn}}\right)$$

$$FV_A = \frac{A}{r_p}\left(\left(1 + r_p\right)^{mn} - 1\right)$$

$$\text{Annuity factor} = \frac{1}{r_p}\left(1 - \frac{1}{\left(1 + r_p\right)^{mn}}\right)$$

Where:

PV_A – Present value of an annuity
A – Annuity amount
r_p – Effective interest rate per period = r/m where m is the number of compounding periods in a year
FV_A – Future value of an annuity
n – Number of years

7. Present Value and Future Value of a growing Annuity

$$PV_{GA} = \frac{A}{r_p - g}\left(1 - \frac{(1+g)^{mn}}{(1+r_p)^{mn}}\right)$$

$$FV_{GA} = \frac{A}{r_p - g}\left((1+r_p)^{mn} - (1+g)^{mn}\right)$$

Where:

PV_A – Present value of an annuity
A – Annuity amount
r_p – Effective interest rate per period = r/m where m is the number of compounding periods in a year
FV_A – Future value of an annuity
n – Number of years
g- Growth rate of the annuity between periods

8. Present Value of a perpetuity without growth and a perpetuity with growth

$$PVp = \frac{A}{r} \qquad \text{(no growth)}$$

$$PVp = \frac{A}{r - g} \qquad \text{(With growth)}$$

Where:
PVp - present value of a perpetuity
A – Perpetuity payments
g – Growth rate of perpetuity payments

9. Net Present Value of an Investment/Project (or series of net cash flows

$$NPV = \sum_{t=0}^{N} \frac{CF_t}{(1+r)^t} = CF_O + \frac{CF_1}{(1+r)} + \frac{CF_2}{(1+r)^2} + ... + \frac{CF_N}{(1+r)^N}$$

Where:

CF_t – The expected net cash flow in period t
r – The discount rate or the investment/projects opportunity cost of capital
N – The investment/projects expected life

10. The internal rate of return of an Investment/Project (or series of net cash flows)

$$0 = \sum_{t=0}^{N} \frac{CF_t}{(1+IRR)^t} = CF_O + \frac{CF_1}{(1+IRR)} + \frac{CF_2}{(1+IRR)^2} + ... + \frac{CF_N}{(1+IRR)^N}$$

The IRR is the discount rate that makes the NPV zero, and is calculated by iteration (trial and error)

11. Time weighted rate of return

$$r_{twr} = [(1+r_1) * (1+r_2) * ... * (1+r_n)] - 1$$

$$r_i = \frac{MV_1 - MV_0}{MV_0}$$

Where r_i is the rate of return for sub-period i that accounts for market value changes after accounting for all cash inflows and cash outflows.

12. Money weighted rate of return

The money weighted rate of return is equivalent to the internal rate of return (IRR) of the cash flows. It is estimated by solving the following equation iteratively (by trial and error):

$$MV_1 = MV_0(1+R)^T + CF_1(1+R)^{(T-t_1)} + ... + CF_n(1+R)^{(T-t_n)}$$

$$r_{mwr} = (1+R)^m - 1$$

Where:

MV_1 – market value at the end of the evaluation period
MV_0 – market value at the beginning of the evaluation period
CF_i – cash flow at period i
T – Length of the evaluation period (e.g. 1 month)
t_i – length of the period from the time of cash flow CF_i to beginning of the period
R- Return per unit of time in the evaluation period
r_{twr} – money weighted rate of return for the whole evaluation period

13. Bank discount yield, r_{BD}

$$r_{BD} = \frac{D}{F}\frac{360}{t}$$

Where:

r_{BD}– annualized bank discount yield
D - The dollar discount, or face value less purchase price (F-P_O)
F – Face value of the T-bill
t- Days remaining to maturity
360 – Bank convention for the number of days in a year

14. Holding period yield, HPY

$$HPY = \frac{P_1 - P_0 + D_1}{P_0}$$

Where:

Po – The initial purchase price of the instrument
P1 – The price received for the instrument at its maturity when sold
D1 – The interest payment received from the instrument at its maturity

15. Effective annual yield, EAY

$$EAY = (1 + HPY)^{(365/t)} - 1$$

16. Money market yield (CD Equivalent yield), r_{MM}

$$r_{MM} = \frac{360 r_{BD}}{360 - (t)(r_{BD})}$$

17. Bond equivalent yield, BEY

$$BEY = Semiannual\ YTM * 2$$

Where:

t- Days remaining to maturity

r_{BD} – bank discount yield

Statistical Concepts

18. Population mean, μ and Sample Mean x-bar

$$\mu = \frac{\sum\limits_{i=1}^{N} X_i}{N} = \frac{X_1 + X_2 + \ldots + X_N}{N}$$

$$\overline{X} = \frac{\sum\limits_{i=1}^{n} X_i}{n} = \frac{X_1 + X_2 + \ldots + X_n}{n}$$

Where:

N – The number of observations in the population
n- The number of observations in the sample
X_i – is i^{th} observation in the population or the sample

19. Weighted mean

$$\overline{X}_w = \sum_{i=1}^{n} w_i X_i$$

Where w_i are weights corresponding to observations X_i and sum of weights is equal to 1

20. The Geometric Mean, G

$$G = (X_1 X_2 X_3 \ldots X_n)^{(1/n)}$$

Where $X_1, X_2,..., X_n$ are the set of n observations for which the geometric mean is to be found.

21. The Geometric Mean return (or compound return), R_G

$$R_G = [(1+R_1)(1+R_2)...(1+R_T)]^{(1/T)} - 1$$

Where $R_1, R_2,... ,R_T$ are holding period returns for sub periods 1, 2, ..., T.

22. The Harmonic Mean

$$\overline{X_H} = \frac{n}{\sum\limits_{i=1}^{n}(1/X_i)} = \frac{n}{(1/X_1)+(1/X_2)+...+(1/X_n)}$$

Where X_i is a set of observations and $X_i > 0$ for all i.

23. Quartiles, Quintiles, Deciles, and Percentiles

L_y, the position of the yth percentile (P_Y), is given by:

$$L_y = (n+1)\frac{y}{100}$$

Where:

y – Is the percentage point at which we are dividing the distribution e.g. 50%

n – Number of observations in sample

Quartiles $Q_1 = P_{25}$; $Q_2 = P_{50}$ = Median; $Q_3 = P_{75}$

The four Quintiles are P_{20}, P_{40}, P_{60} and P_{80}

The Deciles are $P_{10}, P_{20}, P_{30}, P_{40}, P_{50}, P_{60}, P_{70}, P_{80}$ and P_{90}

24. The Range

Range = Maximum value – Minimum value

25. The Mean Absolute Deviation, MAD

$$MAD = \frac{\sum\limits_{i=1}^{n} \left| X_i - \overline{X} \right|}{n} = \frac{\left(X_1 - \overline{X}\right) + \left(X_2 - \overline{X}\right) + ... + \left(X_n - \overline{X}\right)}{n}$$

$\overline{X}$ is the sample mean and n is the number of observations in the sample

26. Population variance, σ^2 and population standard deviation, σ

$$\sigma^2 = \frac{\sum\limits_{i=1}^{N} \left(X_i - \mu\right)^2}{N}$$

$$\sigma = \sqrt{\frac{\sum\limits_{i=1}^{N} \left(X_i - \mu\right)^2}{N}}$$

Where μ is the population mean, X_i are the observations in the population and N is the number of observations that make up the population.

27. Sample variance, s^2 and sample standard deviation, s

$$s^2 = \frac{\sum\limits_{i=1}^{n} \left(X_i - \overline{X}\right)^2}{n-1}$$

$$s = \sqrt{\frac{\sum_{i=1}^{n} \left(X_i - \overline{X}\right)^2}{n-1}}$$

Where $\overline{X}$ is the sample mean, X_i is are the observations in the sample and n is the number of observations that make up the sample from the population.

28. Semi variance, Semi deviation, Target semi variance and Target Semi deviation

Semivariance $= \dfrac{\sum_{i=1}^{n} \left(X_i - \overline{X}\right)^2}{n-1}$

For all $X_i < \overline{X}$

Semideviation is square root of semivariance

Target Semivariance $= \dfrac{\sum_{i=1}^{n} \left(X_i - B\right)^2}{n-1}$

For all $X_i < B$

Where B Is the target value and n is the number of observations.

Target Semideviation is the square root of Target semivariance.

29. Chebyshev's Inequality

The proportion of observations between k standard deviations of the mean is at least

$1 - (1/k^2)$

For all k>1.

30. Coefficient of Variation, CV

$$CV = \frac{s}{\overline{X}}$$

Where s is the sample standard deviation and $\overline{X}$ is the sample mean.

31. The Sharpe Ratio, S_h

$$S_h = \frac{\overline{R_p} - \overline{R_F}}{s_p}$$

Where $\overline{R_p}$ is the mean portfolio return, $\overline{R_F}$ is the risk free rate of return and s_p portfolio standard deviation of returns.

32. Sample Skewness (or Sample relative skewness), S_K

$$SK = \left[\frac{n}{(n-1)(n-2)}\right] \frac{\sum\limits_{i=1}^{n} \left(X_i - \overline{X}\right)^3}{s^3} \approx \left(\frac{1}{n}\right) \frac{\sum\limits_{i=1}^{n} \left(X_i - \overline{X}\right)^3}{s^3}$$

Where n is the number of observations in the sample, X_i are the individual observations, $\overline{X}$ is the sample mean, and s is the sample standard deviation. The approximation is appropriate for large n, and sample skewness is approximated by the mean-cubed deviation.

33. Sample Kurtosis, K and Sample Excess Kurtosis, K_E

$$K = \left(\frac{n(n+1)}{(n-1)(n-2)(n-3)}\right) \frac{\sum\limits_{i=1}^{n} \left(X_i - \overline{X}\right)^4}{s^4}$$

$$K_E = K - \frac{3(n-1)^2}{(n-2)(n-3)} \approx \frac{1}{n} \frac{\sum\limits_{i=1}^{n} (X_i - \overline{X})^4}{s^4} - 3$$

Where n is the number of observations in the sample, s is the sample standard deviation and $\overline{X}$ is the sample mean. The approximation is appropriate for large n.

Probability Concepts

34. Sum of probabilities

If events E_1, E_2, ... , E_n are mutually exclusive (i.e. only one event can occur at a time) and completely exhaustive (i.e. Covers all possible n events), then

P (E_1) + P (E_2) + ... + P (E_n) =1   [sum of probabilities equals 1]

Where $0 \leq P(E_i) \leq 1$ for i from 1 to n

35. Probabilities as odds and odds as probabilities

Given a probability of an event E, P (E), then the odds of that event happening or against is given by:

$$Odds of E = \frac{P(E)}{1 - P(E)}$$

$$Odds against E = \frac{1 - P(E)}{P(E)}$$

Given odds for event E of "a t o b", the implied probability of event E happening is given by:

$$P_{imp}(E) = \frac{a}{a+b}$$

The implied probability of event (s) other than E happening is given by:

$$P_{imp}(NotE) = \frac{b}{a+b}$$

36. Conditional Probability

$$P(A|B) = P(AB) / P(B) \quad P(B) \neq 0$$

Where P (A|B) is the probability of A given that B has occurred, P (AB) is joint probability of A and B occurring and P (B) is the probability of B occurring.

37. Multiplication Rule

$$P(AB) = P(A|B) * P(B) = P(BA) = P(B|A) * P(A)$$

38. Addition Rule

$$P(A \text{ or } B) = P(A) + P(B) - P(AB)$$

39. Independent Events

Two events A and B are independent if and only if (iff):

$$P(A | B) = P(A) \text{ or } P(B|A) = P(B)$$

40. Multiplication Rule for independent events

$$P(AB) = P(A) P(B) = P(BA) = P(B) P(A)$$

This generalizes to more than 2 events   e.g. P (ABCDE) = P (A) P (B) P(C) P (D) P (E)

41. Total Probability Rule

$$P(A) = P(AS_1) + P(AS_2) + ... + P(AS_n) = P(A|S_1)P(S_1) + P(A|S_2)P(S_2) + ... + P(A|S_n)P(S_n)$$

Where S_1, S_2, ..., S_n are mutually exclusive and completely exhaustive events

$$P(A) = P(AS) + P(AS^C) = P(A|S)\, P(S) + P(A|S^C)\, P(S^C)$$

Where $P(S) + P(S^c) = 1$ and S^C is the complement event of S, or the event not S.

42. Expected Value, E(X)

$$E(X) = \sum_{i=1}^{n} P(X_i)X_i = P(X_i)X_i + P(X_2)X_2 + ... + P(X_n)x_n$$

43. Variance, Var(X) or $\sigma^2(X)$

$$\sigma^2(X) = \sum_{i=1}^{n} P(X_i)\big[X_i - E(X)\big]^2 = P(X_1)\big[X_1 - E(X)\big]^2 +$$
$$P(X_2)\big[X_2 - E(X)\big]^2 + ... + P(X_n)\big[X_n - E(X)\big]^2$$

44 Conditional Expected Value, E (X|S)

$$E(X|S) = P(X_1|S)\, X_1 + P(X_2|S)\, X_2 + ... + P(X_n|S)\, X_n$$

E (X|S) is the expected value of a random variable X given an event S.

45. Total Probability Rule for Expected Value, E (X)

$$E(X) = E(X|S_1)\, P(S_1) + E(X|S_2)\, P(S_2) + ... + E(X_n|S_n)\, P(S_n)$$
$$E(X) = E(X|S)\, P(S) + E(X|S^C)\, P(S^C)$$

Where S_1, S_2, ..., S_n are mutually exclusive events and S^c is the event "not S".

46. Expected return of a portfolio, E (R_p)

$$E (R_p) = w_1 E (R_1) + w_2 E (R_2) + ... + w_n E (R_n)$$

Where w_i is the weight of asset i in the portfolio and E (R_i) is the expected return of asset i. This is a weighted average return.

47. Covariance, Cov(X, Y)

Given two random variables X and Y, the covariance between them is given by:

$$Cov (X, Y) = E [\{X - E(X)\} \{Y - E(Y)\}]$$

Covariance between random variables R_A and R_B is given by:

$$Cov\left(R_A, R_B\right) = \sum_i \sum_j P\left(R_{A,i}, R_{B,j}\right) * \left(R_{A,i} - E(R_A)\right) * \left(R_{B,j} - E(R_B)\right)$$

48. The variance of a portfolio, σ^2 (R_p)

$$\sigma^2\left(R_p\right) = \sum_{i=1}^{n} \sum_{j=1}^{n} w_i w_j Cov\left(R_i, R_j\right)$$

For a two asset portfolio, assets 1 and 2, the portfolio variance is given by:

$$\sigma^2\left(R_p\right) = w_1^2 \sigma_1^2 + w_2^2 \sigma_2^2 + 2 w_1 w_2 Cov\left(R_1, R_2\right)$$

For a three asset portfolio, assets 1 and 2, the portfolio variance is given by:

$$\sigma^2\left(R_p\right) = w_1{}^2\sigma_1{}^2 + w_2{}^2\sigma_2{}^2 + w_3{}^2\sigma_3{}^2 + 2\,w_1 w_2 \mathrm{Cov}\left(R_1, R_2\right)$$
$$+ 2\,w_1 w_3 \mathrm{Cov}\left(R_1, R_3\right) + 2\,w_2 w_3 \mathrm{Cov}\left(R_2, R_3\right)$$

Where w_i is the weight of asset i and σ_i is the standard deviation of the returns on asset i.

49. Correlation coefficient, ρ_{ij} between two assets, i and j

$$\rho_{ij} = \frac{\mathrm{Cov}\left(R_i, R_j\right)}{\sigma_i \sigma_j}$$

Where σ_i is the standard deviation of returns for asset i. The correlation coefficient is a measure of linear association between the returns of two assets and ranges between -1 (perfect negative association) and 1 (perfect positive association). A correlation of zero shows no linear relationship.

50. Bayes' Theorem

$$P(Event \mid Information) = \frac{P(Information \mid Event)}{P(Information)} P(Event)$$

Where P (information) >0 and P (Event) and P (Information) are prior probabilities or marginal probabilities.

51. Multiplication rule on counting

If one task can be done in n_1 ways, the second task in n_2 ways given the first and so on for k tasks, the number of ways the k tasks can be done is given by:

$(n_1)(n_2)\ (n_3)\ \dots\ (n_k)$

52. n Factorial (n!)

The number of ways that n objects can be arranged in different ways (e.g. arranged in a line) is given by:

$n! = (n)\ (n-1)\ (n-2)\dots\ (2)(1)$

53. Multinomial Formula (Labeling Problems)

The number of ways in which n objectives can be separated into k different bins (or k different labels) such that n_1 objects go into the first bin, n_2 into the second up till n_k into the kth bin, with $n_1+n_2+...+n_k = n$, is given by:

$$\frac{n!}{n_1!n_2!...n_k!}$$

54. Combination Formula (Binomial Problem)

The number of ways of choosing r objects from a total of n objects in which the order in which the r objects are chosen does not matter is given by:

$$_nC_r = \frac{n!}{(n-r)!r!} \qquad _nC_r = n! / [(n-r)!\ r!]$$

55. Permutation Formula

The number of ways of choosing r objects from a total of n objects in which the order in which the r objects are chosen matters is given by:

$$_nP_r = \frac{n!}{(n-r)!}$$

56. Binomial Distribution

Let X be a random variable that is fully described by n and p, where the n trials are independent and the probability of success is constant for all trials at p. With n = 1, the distribution is a Bernoulli distribution, and with n>1, we have a Binomial distribution. X is described as X~B (n, p). The probability of success in n trials is given by:

$$p(x) = P(X=x) = \frac{n!}{(n-x)!x!}p^x(1-p)^{n-x}$$

57. Mean and variance of the Bernoulli and Binomial distributions

The mean of a Bernoulli distribution B (1, p) is given by:

Mean = p   ;   Variance = p (1-p)

The mean of a Binomial distribution B (n, p) is given by:

Mean = np   ;   Variance = np (1-p)

58. Probability Density function, pdf (uniform distribution), f(x)

f(x) = 1 / (b-a)   For a<x<b   and 0 otherwise

59. Cumulative Distribution function, cdf (uniform distribution), F(x)

F(x) = 0   **for x ≤ a**

F(x) = (x-a) / (b-a)   **for a < x < b**

F(x) = 1   **for x ≥ b**

60. Area under the curve of a pdf, f(x) from a to b

$$P(a \le X \le b) = \int_a^b f(x)dx$$

61. Mean, μ and variance, σ² for a continuous uniform random variable

μ = (a + b)/2   ;   σ²= (b-a) ²/12

62. The Normal density function, f(x)

$$f(x) = \frac{1}{\sigma\sqrt{2\pi}} \exp\left(\frac{-(x-\mu)^2}{2\sigma^2}\right) \quad \text{For } -\infty < x < +\infty$$

Approximately 50% of observations lie between $\mu \pm 0.667\sigma$

Approximately 68% of observations lie between $\mu \pm \sigma$

Approximately 95% of observations lie between $\mu \pm 2\sigma$

Approximately 99% of observations lie between $\mu \pm 3\sigma$

When mean, $\mu=0$ and standard deviation, $\sigma=1$, we have the standard normal distribution (or unit normal distribution).

63. The standard normal random variable, Z

$$Z = (X - \mu) / \sigma$$

Where X is the random variable, μ is the population mean and σ is the population standard deviation.

64. Price relative and continuously compounded returns

Given a beginning price S_0 and ending price S_1, the price relative is given by:

$$S_1/S_0 = 1 + R_{0,1}$$

Where $R_{0,1}$ is the holding period return between periods 0 and 1.

The continuously compounded return, $r_{0,1}$, is given by

$$r_{0,1} = \ln(S_1/S_0) = \ln(1 + R_{0,1})$$

Given multiple time periods between period 0 and T, return over time T, $r_{0,T}$ is given by:

$$r_{0,T} = r_{0,1} + r_{0,2} + \ldots + r_{T-2,T-1} + r_{T-1,T}$$

Assuming that returns over a sub period are independent and identically distributed (IID) with mean, μ and standard deviation σ, then the expected return over the period 0 to T is given by:

$$E(r_{0,T}) = E(r_{0,1}) + E(r_{0,2}) + \ldots + E(r_{T-2,T-1}) + E(r_{T-1,T}) = \mu T$$

And variance is given by:

$$\sigma^2(r_{0,T}) = \sigma^2(r_{0,1}) + \sigma^2(r_{0,2}) + \ldots + \sigma^2(r_{T-2,T-1}) + \sigma^2(r_{T-1,T}) = \sigma^2 T$$

Sampling and Estimation

65. Standard error of the sample mean

The population standard deviation, σ may be known, or estimated by its estimator, s, the sample standard deviation. Then, the standard error of the sample mean is give by:

$$\sigma_{\bar{x}} = \frac{\sigma}{\sqrt{n}} \quad \text{When } \sigma \text{ is known or by } \quad s_{\bar{x}} = \frac{s}{\sqrt{n}} \quad \text{when s is estimated}$$

66. Confidence intervals, CI

Confidence intervals can be estimated from a z or t distributions. In general, the z statistic is used if it is known that the distribution is normal, the sample is large, and the variance is known. Otherwise a t-test is used. When the variance, σ, is unknown, the estimator, s, is used instead. Confidence intervals, CI, are given by either of the following equations:

$$CI : \overline{X} \pm z_{\alpha/2} \frac{\sigma}{\sqrt{n}}$$

$$CI : \overline{X} \pm z_{\alpha/2} \frac{s}{\sqrt{n}}$$

$$CI : \overline{X} \pm t_{\alpha/2,v} \frac{s}{\sqrt{n}}$$

Where α is the significance level or $(1-\alpha)$ is the confidence level, v is the degrees of freedom of the test $(n-1)$ and $z_{\alpha/2}$ and $t_{\alpha/2}$ are z and t statistics read from the z or t tables depending on α and v.

For z, $z_{0.005} = 2.58$, **$z_{0.025} = 1.96$ (the most common for 95% confidence level),** $z_{0.05} = 1.65$

Hypothesis Testing

67. Test statistic

A hypothesis test has a null hypothesis, H_O, and an alternate hypothesis, H_1. The test statistic to perform the hypothesis test is given by:

Test Statistic = (Sample statistic – Value of population parameter under H_O) / Standard error of the sample statistic

Two types of errors are made in hypothesis testing. A type I error is rejecting a true null hypothesis while a type II error is not rejecting a false null hypothesis.

68. Test statistic for hypothesis test of population mean

$$t_{n-1} = \frac{\overline{X} - \mu_0}{s/\sqrt{n}}$$

For unknown population variance and either the sample is large or approximately normally distributed small sample

$$z = \frac{\overline{X} - \mu_0}{\sigma/\sqrt{n}}$$

For known population variance, σ^2, where population is normally distributed

$$z = \frac{\overline{X} - \mu_0}{s/\sqrt{n}}$$

For unknown population variance and large sample as an alternative to the t-test (s is sample standard deviation)

Where t_{n-1} is the t-statistic with n-1 degrees of freedom (n observations in total), $\overline{X}$ is the sample mean and μ_0 is the hypothesized value of population mean.

69. *Test statistic for difference between two means (variances unknown but assumed equal)*

$$t = \frac{\left(\overline{X_1} - \overline{X_2}\right) - \left(\mu_1 - \mu_2\right)}{\left(\frac{s_p^2}{n_1} + \frac{s_p^2}{n_2}\right)^{1/2}}$$

Where $s_p^2 = \frac{(n_1 - 1)s_1^2 + (n_2 - 1)s_2^2}{n_1 + n_2 - 2}$ is a pooled estimator of the common variance and the

degrees of freedom is $n_1 + n_2 - 2$.

70. *Test statistic for difference between two means (variances unknown but assumed unequal)*

$$t = \frac{(\overline{X_1} - \overline{X_2}) - (\mu_1 - \mu_2)}{\left(\dfrac{s_1^2}{n_1} + \dfrac{s_2^2}{n_2} \right)^{1/2}}$$

Where the degree of freedom, df, is modified and is given by:

$$df = \frac{\left(\dfrac{s_1^2}{n_1} + \dfrac{s_2^2}{n_2} \right)^2}{\dfrac{\left(s_1^2/n_1\right)^2}{n_1} + \dfrac{\left(s_2^2/n_2\right)^2}{n_2}}$$

n_1, n_2 are the number of observations is samples 1 and 2, s_1, s_2 are the standard deviations of samples 1 and 2 and (μ_1 - μ_2) is the hypothesized difference between the population means.

71. Test concerning mean differences, $\overline{d}$

$$\overline{d} = \frac{1}{n} \sum_{i=1}^{n} d_i$$

Where n is the number of pairs of observations and $\overline{d}$ is the mean difference. The sample variance is given by:

$$s_d^2 = \frac{\sum_{i=1}^{n} \left(d_i - \overline{d}\right)^2}{n - 1}$$

The sample standard deviation is s_d, the square root of the variance. The standard error of the mean difference $s_{\overline{d}}$ is given by:

$$s\overline{d} = \frac{sd}{\sqrt{n}}$$

The test statistic, $t_{\overline{d}}$, is given by:

$$t_{\overline{d}} = \frac{\overline{d} - \mu_{d0}}{s\overline{d}}$$

With n-1 degrees of freedom, where n is the number of paired observations and μ_{do} is the hypothesized value of mean difference.

72. Test concerning a single variance

We can test whether the variance of a population σ^2 is statistically different, equal to or greater than a hypothesized difference σ_0^2

We can summarize the null (H_O) and alternate (H_a) hypothesis for the two-tailed and one-tailed tests as:

1. H_O: $\sigma^2 = \sigma_0^2$ versus H_a: $\sigma^2 \neq \sigma_0^2$ (two tailed test)

2. H_O: $\sigma^2 = \sigma_0^2$ versus H_a: $\sigma^2 > \sigma_0^2$ (one tailed test)

3. H_O: $\sigma^2 = \sigma_0^2$ versus H_a: $\sigma^2 < \sigma_0^2$ (one tailed test)

The test statistic is a chi-square statistic with n-1 degrees of freedom given by:

$$\chi^2 = \frac{(n-1)s^2}{\sigma_0^2}$$

73. Test concerning the equality or inequality of two variances

We can test whether the variance of a population σ_1^2 is statistically different, equal to or greater than the variance of another population σ_2^2.

We can summarize the null (H_O) and alternate (H_a) hypothesis for the two-tailed and one-tailed tests as:

1. H_O: $\sigma_1^2 = \sigma_2^2$ versus H_a: $\sigma_1^2 \neq \sigma_2^2$ (two tailed test)

2. H_O: $\sigma_1^2 = \sigma_2^2$ versus H_a: $\sigma_1^2 > \sigma_2^2$ (one tailed test)

3. H_O: $\sigma_1^2 = \sigma_2^2$ versus H_a: $\sigma_1^2 < \sigma_2^2$ (one tailed test)

The test statistic is an F statistic with (n-1) degrees of freedom for the numerator and (n-1) degrees of freedom for the denominator given by:

$$F = \frac{s_1^2}{s_2^2}$$

The normal convention is to label the sample 1 with the higher variance so that the F statistic is >1. Thus only the right hand values of the F tables are required to reject or not reject the null hypothesis.

74. Test concerning correlation: The Spearman rank correlation coefficient, r_s

$$r_s = 1 - \frac{6 \sum_{i=1}^{n} d_i^2}{n(n^2 - 1)}$$

Where d_i is the difference between the ranks of each pair of observations on X and Y and n is the number of pair wise observations.

For small samples for which n ≤30, the critical value of the test is given in tables, otherwise a t-test is conducted with (n-2) degrees of freedom with critical value, t, given by:

$$t = \frac{(n-2)^{1/2} \, r_s}{\left(1 - r_s^2\right)^{1/2}}$$

Technical analysis

75. Price target for Head and Shoulders Pattern

Price target = Neckline – (Head – Neckline)

76. Price target for an inverse Head and Shoulders Pattern

Price target = Neckline + (Neckline – Head)

77. Momentum or Rate of Change Oscillator (ROC), M

$$M = (V - V_x) \times 100$$

Where M is the momentum oscillator value, V is the last closing price and V_x is the closing price x days ago (typically 10 days). An alternative method is to have the oscillator oscillates above and below 100. Then, the oscillator, M is given by:

$$M = (V/ V_x) \times 100$$

78. Relative Strength Index, RSI

$$RSI = 100 - \frac{100}{(1 + RS)}$$

Where RS is given by

$$RS = \frac{\Sigma(\text{Up changes for the period under consideration})}{\Sigma(|\text{Down changes for the period under consideration}|)}$$

79. Stochastic Oscillator

Composed of two lines %K and %D given by:

$$\%K = 100\left(\frac{C - L14}{H14 - L14}\right)$$

Where C is the latest closing price, L14 is the lowest price in the last 14 days and H14 is the highest price in the last 14 days. L14 and H14 could be change to say L20 and H20 where the reference days are now 20 rather than 14.

%D = average of the last three %k values calculated daily

80. Short interest ratio

Short interest ratio = Short interest / Average daily trading volume

81. Arms Index or short-term trading index

$$\text{Arms Index} = \frac{\text{Number of advancing issues} \div \text{Number of declining issues}}{\text{Volume of advancing issues} \div \text{Volume of declining issues}}$$

2. ECONOMICS

1. Price Elasticity of Demand, PED

PED =   Percentage change in quantity demanded /   Percentage change in price

PED is always negative, because as price increases quantity demanded decreases and vice versa according to the law of demand, although PED may be reported in absolute value (i.e. ignoring the sign). When PED>|1|, demand is elastic, when PED =|1|demand is unit elastic and when PED <|1|, demand is inelastic. (Note: |x| is absolute value of x).

2. Cross Price Elasticity of Demand, XED

XED = Percentage change in quantity demanded for good A / Percentage change in price of good B

Goods A and B could be substitutes or complements. If substitutes, XED is positive. If complements, XED is negative.

3. Income Elasticity of Demand, IED

IED = Percentage change in quantity demanded / Percentage change in income

IED could be positive or negative. When positive and less than 1 (income inelastic), we have a normal good. When positive and greater than 1 (income elastic), we have a normal good that can be classified a luxury good. When less than zero (i.e. negative IED), the good is classified as an inferior good.

4. Price Elasticity of Supply, PES

PES = Percentage change in quantity supplied / Percentage change in price

If PES is zero, we have perfectly inelastic supply (i.e. supply is constant whatever the price). When PES is infinite, we have perfectly elastic supply (i.e. all supply is at a particular price).

5. The Four firm Concentration Ratio, CR_4

Given the market share of the top four firms in an industry as MS_1, MS_2, MS_3 & MS_4, the four firm concentration ratio CR_4 is given by:

$$CR_4 = MS_1 + MS_2 + MS_3 + MS_4$$

6. The Herfindahl-Hirschman Index, HHI

The Herfindahl-Hirschman Index is the sum of the market shares of the 50 largest firms in an industry and is given by:

$$HHI = \sum_{i=1}^{N \leq 50} MS_i^2$$

Where MS_i is the market share of firm i and where the sum is done over the number of firms in the industry if less than 50.

Costs

7. Total Costs, TC

TC = TFC + TVC   [TOTAL COST = TOTAL FIXED COST + TOTAL VARIABLE COST]

8. Marginal Cost, MC

MC = ΔTC / ΔQ

Change in total cost resulting from a change in output, Q

9. Average Fixed Cost, AFC

AFC = TFC / Q   (Total fixed cost per unit of output)

10. Average Variable Cost, AVC

AVC = TVC / Q   (Total variable cost per unit of output)

11. Average Fixed Cost, AFC

ATC = TC / Q = AFC + AVC   (Total cost per unit of output)

12. Total Revenue, TR

TR= P * Q (Price x Quantity)   (or TR=P*TP) Where TP is total Product

13. Marginal Revenue, MR

MR= ΔTR / ΔQ

Change in total revenue resulting from a one unit increase in quantity.

14. Economic Profit, π

π = TR - TC

15. Marginal Analysis

MR = MC   (For profit-maximising output)

Market for Factors of Production

16. Marginal Product, MP

MP = ΔTP/ ΔL

Change in total product (TP) resulting from one unit increase in the quantity of labour employed (L).

17. Marginal Revenue Product, MRP

MRP = MR x MP = (ΔTR/ ΔTP) x (ΔTP/ ΔL) = ΔTR/ΔL

Change in total revenue (TR) resulting from one unit increase in the quantity of labour employed (L).

18. Two equivalent conditions for profit maximization

MR = MC　　or　MRP = W (wage rate)

MR = MRP/MP and MC=W/MP

19. Marginal Revenue Product of Capital, MRPC

MRPC = ΔTR/ΔC

Change in total revenue (TR) resulting from one unit increase in the quantity of capital (C).

Economic Indicators & Money

20. Unemployment rate

Unemployment rate　= (Number of people unemployed / Labor Force) * 100%

21. Labor Force

Labor Force = Number of people employed + Number of people unemployed

22. *Labor force Participation rate*

Labor force participation rate   =   (Labor Force / Working population) * 100%

23. *Employment-to Population ratio*

Employment-to-population ratio = Number of people employed / Working-age population

24. *Aggregate hours*

Aggregate hours = Total Full time hours per year + Total Part time hours per year

25. *Real wage rate*

Real wage rate   =   Money (or Nominal) wage rate (dollars per hour) /   Price Level

26. *CPI*

CPI = Cost of CPI basket at current period prices / Cost of CPI basket at base period prices

27. *Inflation rate*

Inflation rate =   (CPI this year – CPI last year) / CPI last year

28. *Aggregate Demand, Y (real GDP)*

$$Y = C + I + G + X - M$$

Where C is real consumption expenditure, I is investment, G is government expenditure, X is exports and M is imports. (X-M) is the real net exports.

29. Money Multiplier, MM

The money multiplier is the ratio of the change in the quantity of money to the change in the monetary base.

MM = 1 / RR = 1/ (1-L)

Where RR is the required reserve ratio (L=1-RR)   and there is no currency drain ratio and desired reserve ratio equals actual reserve ratio

MM = (1+a)/ (1+b)

Where a is the currency drain ratio and b is the desired reserve ratio

30. The equation of exchange

P = M *(V/Y)

Where P is the price level, M is the quantity of money, V is the velocity of money and Y is the real GDP. This shows a change in quantity of money M, results in a proportional growth in price level, P.

31. The inflation rate in terms of money and GDP growth rate

Inflation rate = money growth rate – real GDP growth rate

32. Budget Balance, BB

BB = Tax revenues – outlays

If BB > 0, we have a budget surplus, if BB <0, we have a budget deficit and BB = 0 is a balanced budget.

33. The Investment equation

Investment = Private savings + Government savings

Where Private savings is savings plus net imports (S + [M-X]) and government savings is net taxes less government expenditure (T-G).

34. The Taylor rule for setting the Federal Funds Rate, FFR

FFR = 2 + INF +0.5(INF-2) + 0.5(GAP)   (in percent)

Where INF is the current inflation rate and GAP is the current output gap (real GDP – potential GDP). This equation assumes that the equilibrium real interest rate is 2%.

3. FINANCIAL REPORTING & ANALYSIS

FINANCIAL STATEMENTS

1. Net Income

Net Income (loss) = Revenue – Expenses

2. Fundamental Accounting Equation

Assets = Liability + Owners Equity

3. Owners' Equity

Owners Equity = Contributed capital + retained earnings

4. Ending retained earnings

Ending retained earnings = Beginning retained earnings + Net income – Dividends

5. Expanded accounting equation

Assets = Liabilities + Contributed capital + Beginning retained earnings + Revenue-Expenses -Dividends

6. Straight Line depreciation

Annual depreciation = (Cost – Residual Value) / Estimated useful life

7. *Diminishing (or declining) balance method*

Annual depreciation = depreciation percentage (straight line)

x acceleration percentage x Net book value

8. *Net Book Value*

Net book value = Asset cost value – Accumulated depreciation

Where accumulated depreciation is the sum of depreciation to date.

9. *Basic Earnings per Share (Basic EPS)*

Basic EPS = (Net Income – Preferred Dividends)/ Weighted average number of shares outstanding

10. *Weighted average number of shares outstanding, N_{WA}*

$$N_{WA} = \sum_{t=0}^{12} N_t \left(\frac{12-t}{12} \right)$$

Where N_t is the number of shares new shares issued (or bought back) in month t, and the equation assumes share transactions are calculated on a monthly basis over a 12 month period.

11. *Diluted Earnings per Share (Diluted EPS) with convertible preferred stock*

Diluted EPS = Net Income / (Weighted average number of shares outstanding +New common shares that could have been issued at conversion)

12. *Diluted EPS with convertible debt*

Diluted EPS = (Net Income +After-tax interest on convertible debt -Preferred dividends)/ (Weighted average number of shares outstanding+ New common shares that could have been issued at conversion)

13. *Diluted EPS with stock options, warrants or their equivalents*

Diluted EPS = (Net Income - Preferred dividends)/(Weighted average number of shares outstanding +New common shares that would have been issued at option exercise -Shares that could have been purchased with cash received upon exercise)

14. *Net profit margin (profit margin or return on sales)*

Net profit margin = Net Income / Revenue

15. *Gross profit margin*

Gross profit margin = Gross profit / Revenue

Where gross profit is revenue less cost of sales (or cost of goods sold).

16. *Return on assets*

Return on assets = Net income / Ending total assets

17. *Return on equity*

Return on equity =   Net income / Average shareholder equity

18. *Comprehensive income*

Comprehensive income = Net income +other comprehensive income

Balance Sheet Liquidity ratios

19. Current ratio

Current ratio = Current asset / Current liabilities

20. Quick (acid test) ratio

Quick ratio = (Cash + Marketable securities +Receivables) / Current liabilities

21. Cash ratio

Cash ratio = (Cash + Marketable securities) / Current liabilities

Balance Sheet Solvency ratios

22. Long-term debt to equity ratio

Long-term debt to equity ratio = Total long-term debt   / Total equity

23. Debt to equity ratio

Debt to equity ratio = Total debt / Total equity

24. Total Debt ratio

Total Debt ratio =   Total debt / Total assets

25. Financial leverage ratio

Financial leverage ratio = Total assets / Total equity

Cash Flow analysis

26. Free Cash Flow to the Firm, FCFF

FCFF = NI + NCC + Int(1-Tax rate) – FCInv – WCInv

FCFF = EBIT (1-Tax rate) + NCC – FCInv – WCInv

FCFF = EBITDA (1-Tax rate) + NCC (Tax rate) – FCInv – WCInv

FCFF = CFO + Int (1-Tax rate) – FCInv

Where NI is Net Income, NCC is non cash charges (e.g. depreciation and amortization), Int is interest expense, FCInv is fixed capital expenditures, WCInv is working capital expenditures, EBIT is earnings before interest and taxes, EBITDA is earning before interest, taxes, depreciation and amortization, and CFO is cash flow from operations.

27. Free Cash Flow to Equity, FCFE

FCFE = NI + NCC – FCInv – WCInv + Net borrowing – Net debt repayment

FCFE = CFO – FCInv + Net borrowing – Net debt repayment

FCFE = EBIT (1-Tax rate)-Int(1-Tax rate) + Dep – FCInv – WCInv + Net borrowing – Net debt repayment

FCFE = EBITDA (1-Tax rate)+Dep(Tax rate) - Int(1-Tax rate) – FCInv – WCInv +Net borrowing – Net debt repayment

FCFE = FCFF – Int(1-Tax rate) + Net borrowing

Cash flow performance ratios

28. Cash flow to revenue ratio

Cash flow to revenue ratio = CFO / Net Revenue

29. *Cash return on assets ratio*

Cash return on assets = CFO / Average total assets

30. *Cash return on equity ratio*

Cash return on equity = CFO / Average shareholders' equity

31. *Cash to income ratio*

Cash to income ratio = CFO / Operating income

32. *Cash flow per share ratio*

Cash flow per share ratio = (CFO – Preferred dividends)/Average number of common shares outstanding

Cash flow coverage ratios

33. *Debt coverage ratio*

Debt coverage ratio   = CFO / Total debt

34. *Interest coverage ratio*

Interest coverage ratio = (CFO + Interest paid +Taxes paid) / Interest paid

35. *Reinvestment ratio*

Reinvestment ratio = CFO / Cash paid for long term assets

36. Debt payment ratio

Debt payment ratio = CFO / Cash paid for long-term debt repayment

37. Dividend payment ratio

Dividend payment ratio = CFO / Dividends paid

38. Investing and financing ratio

Investing and financing ratio = CFO / Cash outflows for investing and financing activities

Inventory ratios

39. Inventory turnover ratio

Inventory turnover ratio = Cost of goods sold / Ending inventory

40. Number of days of inventory

Number of days of inventory = 365 days / Inventory turnover ratio

41. LIFO Reserve

LIFO Reserve = FIFO inventory value – LIFO inventory value

Inventory is reported at lower of cost or net realizable value according to US GAAP and IFRS.

42. *Price to Earnings ratio (P/E ratio)*

P/E ratio = Price per share / Earnings per share

43. *Price to Operating Cash flow per share ratio (P/CFO ratio)*

P/CFO = Price per share / Operating cash flow per share

44. *Enterprise value/EBITDA ratio (EV/EBITDA ratio)*

EV/EBITDA = Enterprise Value / Earnings before interest, taxes, depreciation and amortization

Enterprise value is the market value of debt, equity, preferred shares, minority interest less cash and cash equivalents

Depreciation Estimates

45. *Historical cost*

Historical cost = Accumulated depreciation + Net PPE

46. *Estimated total useful life*

Estimated total useful life = Estimated age of equipment + Estimated remaining life

Where Estimated total useful life = Historical cost/annual depreciation expense, Estimated age of equipment = Accumulated depreciation/annual depreciation expense and Estimated remaining life = Net PPE/annual depreciation expense.

47. *Gain or loss on asset sale*

Gain (loss) on asset sale = Cash collected from sale (sale proceeds) - Carrying value of asset at time of sale (Net book value)

48. Goodwill impairment loss

Goodwill impairment loss = Book value of Goodwill - Implied value of goodwill

Book value of goodwill is the acquisition price less net assets of company acquired. Implied book value of goodwill is the fair value of the company less fair value of company net assets at any point in time.

Income Taxes

49. Reported effective tax rate

Reported effective tax rate = Income tax expense / Pretax income

50. Deferred tax liability (asset)

Deferred tax liability (asset) = applicable tax rate x (Asset carrying value – asset tax base)

Amortizing a bond premium or discount

51. Interest payment

Interest payment = bond coupon rate x Bond face value

52. Interest expense (effective interest method)

Interest expense$_t$ =Historical market rate x BV (Bond)$_t$

Where BV (Bond)$_t$ is the bond book value at time t and the interest expense is recorded at same time. The starting book value of the bond, BV_0 is the present value of the bond at the onset (amount raised on bond issue.

53. Amortized amount (effective interest method)

Amortized amount$_t$ = Interest expense$_t$ - Interest payment

54. Bond book value, BV (Bond)$_t$

BV (Bond)$_{t+1}$ = BV (Bond)$_t$ + Amortized amount

At maturity, the Bond book value is equal to the face value of the bond.

55. Amortized amount (Straight-line method)

Amortized amount = (Bond Face value – BV$_0$) / Term to maturity

This amount is a constant over the term of the bond.

56. Interest expense (Straight-line method)

Interest expense = Interest payment / Amortized amount (straight line)

Accounting ratios

57. Activity ratios

Inventory turnover = Cost of goods sold / average inventory

Days of inventory on hand (DOH) = number of days in period / inventory turnover

Receivables turnover = Revenue / average receivables

Days of sales outstanding (DSO) = Number of days in period / receivables turnover

Payables turnover = Purchases / average trade payables

Number of days of payables = Number of days in period / payables turnover

Working capital turnover = Revenue / average working capital

Fixed asset turnover = Revenue / average net fixed assets

Total asset turnover = Revenue / average total assets

58. Liquidity ratios

Current ratio = Current assets / Current liabilities

Quick ratio = (Cash + short-term marketable securities + receivables) / Current liabilities

Cash ratio = (Cash + short-term marketable securities) / Current liabilities

Defensive interval ratio = (Cash + short-term marketable securities + receivables) /Daily cash expenditures

Cash conversion cycle (net operating cycle) = Days on inventory on hand (DOH) + Days of sales outstanding (DSO) –Number of days payable

59. Solvency ratios (Debt ratios)

Debt-to-assets ratio = Total debt / Total assets

Debt-to-capital ratio = Total debt / (Total debt + Total shareholders' equity)

Debt-to-equity ratio = Total debt / Total shareholders' equity

Financial leverage ratio = Average total assets / Average total equity

Total debt refers to interest bearing short and long term debt

60. Solvency ratios (Coverage ratios)

Interest coverage = Earnings before interest and taxes (EBIT) / Interest payments

Fixed charge coverage = [Earnings before interest and taxes (EBIT) + lease payments]/ [Interest payments + lease payments]

Profitability Ratios

61. Return on sales

Gross profit margin = Gross profit / Revenue

Operating profit margin = Operating income (or EBIT) / Revenue

Pre-tax margin = Earnings before tax but after interest (EBT) / revenue

Net profit margin = Net income / Revenue

62. Return on Investment

Return on total capital = EBIT / (Total debt + Equity)

Return on equity (ROE) = Net income / Average shareholders' equity

Return on common equity = (Net income-Preferred dividends) / Average common equity

Return on assets (ROA) = Net income / Average total assets

Operating return on asset (OROA) = Operating income / Average total assets

63. DuPont analysis

ROE = Net income/Average shareholders' equity
     = (Net income/Average total assets) x (Average Total assets/Average Shareholders' equity)

ROE = ROA x Leverage

ROE= (Net income/ Revenue) x (Revenue/Average total assets)
     x (Average total assets/Average shareholders' equity)

ROE = Net profit margin x Asset turnover x Leverage

ROE = (Net income/EBT) x (EBT/EBIT) x (EBIT/Revenue) x (Revenue/Average total assets)
        x (Average Total assets/Average Shareholders' equity)

ROE = Tax burden x Interest burden x EBIT margin x Asset turnover x Leverage

64. Valuation ratios

Price-to-Earnings ratio (P/E) = Price per share / Earnings per share

Price-to-Cashflow ratio (P/CF) = Price per share / Cashflow per share

Price-to-Sales ratio (P/S) = Price per share / Sales per share

Price-to-Book value ratio (P/S) = Price per share / Book value of equity per share

65. Per-share quantities

EBITDA per share = EBITDA / Average number of shares outstanding

Dividends per share = Common dividends declared / Weighted average number of ordinary shares outstanding

66. Dividend related quantities

Dividend payout ratio = Common share dividends / Net income attributable to common shares

Retention rate (b) = (Net income attributable to common shares – Common share dividends)/ (Net income attributable to common shares)

Sustainable growth rate = Retention rate x Return on equity = b x ROE

Industry-specific ratios

67. Business Risk

Coefficient of variation of operating income = Standard deviation of operating income/Average operating income

Coefficient of variation of net income = Standard deviation of net income/Average net income

Coefficient of variation of revenue = Standard deviation of revenue/Average revenue

68. Financial Sector Ratios

Capital adequacy-banks = various components of capital/ Risk-weighted assets, market risk exposure, and level of operational risk assumed

Monetary reserve requirement = Reserves held at central bank / Specified deposit liabilities

Liquid asset requirement =Approved "readily marketable" securities / Specified deposit liabilities

Net interest margin =Net interest income / Total interest-earning assets

69. Retail Ratios

Same (or comparable) store sales = Average revenue growth year over year for stores open for both periods

Sales per square foot (meter) =Revenue/ Total retail space in feet or meters

70. Service companies

Revenue per employee = Revenue / Total number of employees

Net income per employee = Net income / Total number of employee

71. Hotel

Average daily rate = Room revenue / Number of rooms sold

Occupancy rate = Number of rooms occupied / Number of rooms available

72. Selected credit ratios (Standard & Poor's)

EBIT interest coverage = EBIT / Gross interest (prior to deductions for capitalized interest or interest income

EBITDA interest coverage = EBITDA / Gross interest (prior to deductions for capitalized interest or interest income

Funds from operations to total debt = Funds from operations (net income adjusted for non-cash items) / Total debt

Free operating cash flow to total debt = Cash flow from operations (adjusted) less capital expenditures / Total debt

Total debt to EBITDA = Total debt / EBITDA

Return on capital = EBIT / Capital (Average common equity and preferred stock and short-term portions of debt, noncurrent deferred taxes and minority interest)

Total debt to total debt plus equity = Total debt / Total debt plus equity

73. Z-score

Z = [1.2x (Current assets – Current liabilities)/Total assets] + 1.4x (Retained earnings/Total assets) + 3.3x (EBIT/Total assets) + 0.6x (Market value of stock/Book value of liabilities) + 1.0x (Sales/Total assets)

74. Segment ratios

Segment margin = Segment profit or loss / Segment revenue

Segment turnover = Segment revenue / Segment assets

Segment ROA = Segment profit or loss / Segment assets

Segment debt ratio = Segment liabilities / Segment assets

75. Goodwill

Goodwill = Amount paid to acquire a company – Fair value of net identifiable assets acquired

4. CORPORATE FINANCE

1. Investment appraisal

Average accounting rate of return = Average net income / Average book value

Profitability index = (Initial investment + NPV) / Initial investment

2. Weighted average cost of capital, WACC

$$WACC = \omega_d r_d (1-t) + \omega_p r_p + \omega_e r_e$$

Where ω_d is the weight of debt in capital structure (D/V), ω_p is the weight of preferred stock (P/V), ω_e is the weight of equity (E/V) and V=D+P+E. r_d is the before tax marginal cost of debt, r_p the marginal cost of preferred stock, r_e is the marginal cost of equity and t is the marginal tax rate.

3. Cost of debt estimate, r_d

$$P_0 = \left(\sum_{t-1}^{n} \frac{PMT_t}{\left(1+\frac{r_d}{2}\right)^t} \right) + \frac{FV}{\left(1+\frac{r_d}{2}\right)^n}$$

Where semi-annual payments are assumed and the cost of debt rd (yield to maturity of bond) is what makes the present value of the bond cash flows equal to its market price. P_o is the current bond market price, PMT_t is the interest payment at period t, FV is the single payment on bond maturity and n is the number of periods to maturity.

4. Cost of preferred stock estimate, r_P

$$r_p = D_p / P_p$$

Where D_p is the preferred stock dividend per share and P_p is the preferred stock market price per share.

Cost of equity estimate, r_e

5. CAPM approach

$$r_e = R_F + \beta_e [E(R_M) - R_F]$$

Where R_F is the risk free rate of return, $E(R_M)$ is the expected market return; β_e is the beta of equity, e, which is a measure of the return sensitivity of a stock to market returns. The difference $E(R_M) - R_F$ is the market risk premium.

6. Multifactor model approach

$$r_e = R_F + \beta_1 \text{ (Factor risk premium)}_1 + \beta_2 \text{ (Factor risk premium)}_2 + \ldots + \beta_J \text{ (Factor risk premium)}_J$$

Where β_i is the stocks sensitivity to factor i and the factor premiums are for respective factors.

7. Dividend discount model (DDM) approach

$$r_e = (D_1/P_0) + g$$

Where D_1 is next year's expected dividend, P_0 is the current share price and g is the sustainable growth rate given by g = retention rate * ROE = (1-payout rate)* ROE

8. Bond yield plus risk premium approach

$$r_e = r_d + \text{Risk premium}$$

The risk premium is additional compensation for bearing equity risk above the before tax cost of debt, r_d.

9. Asset Beta, β_a (no taxes)

$$\beta_a = \omega_d\beta_d + \omega_e\beta_e = [D/(D+E)]\,\beta_d + [E/(D+E)]\,\beta_e$$

Where ω_d and ω_e are the weights of debt and equity and β_d and β_e are debt are equity betas.

10. Asset Beta, β_a (with tax rate, t) and assuming zero debt beta

$$\beta_a = \beta_e\left[\dfrac{1}{1+\left(\left(1-t\right)\dfrac{D}{E}\right)}\right]$$

11. Equity Beta, β_e (with tax rate, t) and assuming zero debt beta

$$\beta_e = \beta_a\left[1+\left(\left(1-t\right)\dfrac{D}{E}\right)\right]$$

12. Country equity premium

Country equity risk premium = sovereign yield spread *(Annualized standard deviation of equity index / Annualized standard deviation of Sovereign bond market in terms of the developed market currency)

13. Break point in raising capital

Break point = Amount of capital at which the source's cost of capital changes / Proportion of new capital raised from the source

14. Costs of equity incorporating floatation

$$r_e = [D_1 / (P_0 - F)] + g$$

$$r_e = [D_1 / \{(P_0(1 - f))\}] + g$$

Where F is the per share floatation costs, f is the floatation costs as a percentage of share issue price, D_1 is the expected dividend next year and g is the sustainable growth rate of dividends.

15. Unlevered beta (Asset beta) for a comparable company, β_{UC}

$$\beta_{UC} = \frac{\beta_{LC}}{\left[1 + \left(\left(1 - t_C\right)\dfrac{DC}{EC}\right)\right]}$$

Where β_{LC} is the beta of a comparable company with the appropriate debt-to-equity ratio D_C/E_C and t_c is the marginal tax rate for the comparable company.

16. Equity beta for a project or company with leverage, β_{LP}

$$\beta_{LP} = \beta_{UC}\left[1 + \left(\left(1 - t_p\right)\dfrac{Dp}{Ep}\right)\right]$$

Where β_{UC} is defined from above, the asset beta for a comparable company, D_p/E_p is the relevant debt-to-equity ratio for the project or company and t_p is the relevant marginal tax rate.

Working Capital Management

17. Money market yield

$$\text{Money markey yield} = \left(\frac{\text{Face value - Purchase price}}{\text{Purchase price}} \right) \left(\frac{360}{\text{Number of days to maturity}} \right)$$

18. Bond equivalent yield

$$\text{Bond equivalent yield} = \left(\frac{\text{Face value - Purchase price}}{\text{Purchase price}} \right) \left(\frac{365}{\text{Number of days to maturity}} \right)$$

19. Discount-basis yield

$$\text{Discount basis yield} = \left(\frac{\text{Face value - Purchase price}}{\text{Face value}} \right) \left(\frac{360}{\text{Number of days to maturity}} \right)$$

20. Float factor

Float factor = Average daily float/Average daily deposit

Where average daily deposit is the total amount of checks deposited/ Number of days.

21. Cost of trade credit

$$\text{cost of trade credit} = \left(1 + \frac{D}{1-D} \right)^{(365/N)} - 1$$

Where D is the discount and N is the number of days beyond the discount period.

22. *Number of days payables*

Number of days payables = Accounts payable / average day's purchases

23. *Cost of borrowing with commitment fee*

Cost = (Interest + Commitment fee) / Loan amount

24. *Cost of borrowing with "all inclusive" rate*

Cost = Interest / Net proceeds = Interest/ (Loan amount – Interest)

25. *Cost of borrowing with dealer fees and other fees*

Cost = (Interest + Dealer's commission + Backup costs)/ (Loan amount – interest)

Portfolio management

26. *After-tax income*

After-tax income return = Pre-tax income return x (1-Marginal tax rate)

27. *Equivalent taxable yield*

Equivalent taxable yield = Municipal yield / (1-Marginal tax rate)

28. *Expected return of a portfolio, R_p*

$$E(R_p) = \sum_{i=1}^{n} \omega_i R_i$$

Where ω_i is the weight of asset i in the portfolio and R_i is the expected return of asset i.

29. *Variance, σ^2 and standard deviation, σ of an individual investment*

$$\sigma^2 = \sum_{i=1}^{n} \left[R_i - E(R_i) \right]^2 P_i$$

$$\sigma = \sqrt{\sigma^2}$$

Where P_i is the probability of return R_i and $E(R_i)$ is the expected rate of return of the investment.

30. *Covariance of rates of return between assets i and j, Cov_{ij}*

$$Cov_{ij} = E \{ [R_i - E(R_i)] [R_j - E(R_j)] \}$$

31. *Single index market model*

$$R_i = a_i + b_i R_m + \varepsilon$$

Where R_i is the return on asset I given by the single market model regression, a_i is an intercept coefficient, b_i is a slope coefficient and R_m is the return for the market.

32. Correlation coefficient between two assets given single index market model, r_{ij}

$$r_{ij} = b_i b_j \frac{\sigma_m^2}{\sigma_i \sigma_j} = \frac{Cov_{ij}}{\sigma_i \sigma_j}$$

Where the slope estimates b_i are from equation for single market model, σ_m is the standard deviation of the market returns and σ_i is the standard deviation of returns for asset i. This reduces the correlation estimates required for calculating portfolio standard deviation assuming the single index market model is a good model to estimate returns.

33. Slope of the efficient frontier in return-risk space (R-σ axis)

Slope = $\Delta E(R_{port})$ / $\Delta E(\sigma_{port})$

The slope decreases as you move up the efficient frontier showing diminishing marginal return to risk.

34. Covariance between two sets of returns with n observations

$$Cov_{ij} = \sum_{i=1}^{n} \frac{[R_{it} - E(R_{it})][R_{jt} - E(R_{jt})]}{n-1}$$

35. Risk measure for the Capital Market Line (CML)

Var (R_{it}) = Var $(b_i R_{Mt})$ + Var(ε) = Systematic variance + Unsystematic variance

Where R_{it} is asset i return for period t, a_i is a regression intercept coefficient, b_i is the regression slope coefficient, R_{Mt} is the market return for period t and ε is a random error in return.

36. *The Security Market Line, SML*

$$E(R_i) = RFR + \frac{Cov_{i,M}}{\sigma_M^2}(R_M - RFR) = RFR + \beta_i(R_M - RFR)$$

37. *Characteristic line of an asset with the market portfolio*

$$R_{i,t} = \alpha_i + \beta_i R_{M,t} + \varepsilon$$

Where $R_{i,t}$ is the return for asset i in period t, α_i is the regression intercept term which is $\overline{R_i} - \beta_i \overline{R_M}$, $R_{M,t}$ is the market return in period t, β_i is the systematic risk measure for asset i equal to covariance of asset i returns and market returns divided by the market return and ε is a random error term.

38. *Zero Beta model*

$$E(R_i) = E(R_z) + \beta_i [E(R_M) - E(R_Z)]$$

Where $E(R_i)$ is expected return of asset i, $E(R_z)$ is expected return of the zero-beta portfolio and $E(R_M)$ is the expected return of the market portfolio. β_i is the systematic risk measure for asset i.

39. *Expected after tax rate of return, E (R_i^{AT})*

$$E(R_i^{AT}) = \frac{[(P_e - P_b)(1 - T_{cg})] + [(Div)(1 - T_i)]}{P_b}$$

Where P_e is ending price, P_b is beginning price, T_{cg} is capital gains tax rate, Div is dividends paid during the period, and T_i is the relevant dividend tax rate.

5. EQUITY INVESTMENTS

Stock market indexes

1. Price-weighted index, Dow Jones Industrial average

$$DJIA_t = \sum_{i=1}^{30} \frac{P_{it}}{D_{adj}}$$

Where $DJIA_t$ is the value of the DJIA on day t, P_{it} is the closing price of stock i on day t and D_{adj} is the adjusted divisor on day t.

2. Value-weighted index

$$Index_t = \frac{\sum P_t Q_t}{\sum P_b Q_b} (beginning\ index\ value)$$

Where $Index_t$ is the index value on day t, P_t and P_b are ending prices (on day t) and price on base day and Qt and Q_b are the number of outstanding or freely floating shares on day t and base day.

3. Abnormal rate of return of a stock, AR_{it}

$$AR_{it} = R_{it} - E (R_{it})$$

Where R_{it} is the actual return for security i during period t and $E (R_{it})$ is the expected return over the same period.

Discounted cash flow valuation

4. Value of an asset, V

$$V = \sum_{t=1}^{n} \frac{CF_t}{(1+r)^t}$$

Where CF_t is the cash flow occurring at time t, r is the relevant discount rate reflecting cash flow risk and n is the asset life. This says that the value of an asset is the present value of the cash flows generated by the asset.

5. The Dividend Discount Model

$$V = \frac{D1}{(1+r)} + \frac{D2}{(1+r)^2} + ... + \frac{D\infty}{(1+r)^\infty} = \sum_{i=1}^{n} \frac{Dt}{(1+r)^n}$$

Where D_i is the dividend paid in period i, r is the required rate of return on the stock and n is assumed to be infinite (stock is perpetuity). '__' refers to missing terms in the series.

6. Constant growth Dividend Discount

$$V = \frac{D0(1+g)}{(1+r)} + \frac{D0(1+g)^2}{(1+r)^2} + ... + \frac{D0(1+g)^n}{(1+r)^n} = \frac{D1}{r-g}$$

Where D_i is the dividend in period i, g is the constant growth rate of dividends in perpetuity, n is the number of periods assumed to be infinite and r is the required rate of return on the stock (discount rate).

7. Present value of operating free cash flows, OCFF (or FCFF).

$$V = \sum_{t=1}^{n} \frac{OCFF_t}{(1+WACC)^t}$$

Where V is the firm value, n is number of periods assumed to be infinite, $OCFF_t$ is the firms operating free cash flow in period t and WACC is the firm's weighted average cost of capital. Assuming a constant growth rate of OCFF of g in infinity, the DDM can be adapted to give:

$$V = \frac{OCFF1}{WACC - g}$$

8. Present value of free cash flows to equity, FCFE

$$V_E = \sum_{t=1}^{n} \frac{FCFE_t}{(1+r)^t}$$

Where VE is the value of the firm's equity, $FCFE_t$ is the free cash flow to equity holders in period t, n is the number of periods assumed to be infinite and r is the firm's cost of equity capital. Assuming a constant growth rate of FCFF of g in infinity, the DDM can be adapted to give:

$$V_E = \frac{FCFE_1}{r-g}$$

Relative valuation techniques

9. Earnings multiplier model

Earnings multiplier = Price/Earnings ratio = P_0/E_1
= Current market price/Expected 12 month forward earnings

$$P_0 = \frac{D_1}{r-g}$$

$$\frac{P_0}{E_1} = \frac{D_1/E_1}{r-g}$$

10. Price-to-cash flow ratio

$$P/CF = \frac{P_t}{CF_{t+1}}$$

Where P/CF is the price to cash flow ratio for the firm (known) and P_t is the price in period t and CF_{t+1} is the expected cash flow in the next period.

11. Price-to-Book ratio

$$P/BV = \frac{P_t}{BV_{t+1}}$$

Where P/BV is the price to book value of equity per share ratio for the firm (known) and P_t is the price in period t and BV_{t+1} is the expected book value of equity per share in the next period.

12. Inflation rate, i from nominal rate, n and real rate, r

$$(1+n) = (1+r)(1+i) \quad ; \quad i = [(1+n)/(1+r)]-1$$

13. Forecasting Earnings per share in period t, EPS$_t$

$$EPS_t = a + bt$$

or

$$\ln(EPS_t) = a + bt$$

Where a is an intercept coefficient from the regression and b is a slope coefficient. The first equation represents EPS change while the second equation represents EPE percentage change. 'ln' stands for natural logarithm.

6. FIXED INCOME

1. *Bond coupon payment*

Coupon payment = Coupon rate x Par Value

2. *Coupon rate on a floating-rate security*

Coupon rate = Reference rate + margin

3. *Inverse floater coupon rate*

Coupon rate = K – (L x Reference rate)

Where K is a fixed rate and L is a coupon leverage multiplier. If L>1, we have a leveraged inverse floater.

4. *Deleveraged floater coupon rate*

Coupon rate = (b x Reference rate) + margin

b is between 0 and 1

5. *Dual-Indexed floater coupon rate*

Coupon rate = (Reference rate$_1$ – Reference rate$_2$) + margin

6. *Price of a callable bond*

Price of a callable bond = Price of an option-free bond – Price of embedded call option

7. *Price of a putable bond*

Price of a putable bond = Price of an option-free bond + Price of embedded call option

8. *Bond Duration, D (approximate percentage price change for 1% change in yield)*

$$D = \frac{V\,down - V\,up}{2(V)(\Delta y)}$$

Where V_{down} is the price if yields decrease, V_{up} is price if yields increase, V is initial bond price and Δy is the yield change in decimals (e.g. 1% =0.01). Note that 1% = 100 basis points.

9. *Dollar Duration, DD (approximate dollar change of a bond position)*

DD = - Duration x Initial Bond price x yield change in decimals = - (D) (V) (Δy)

10. *Fixed monthly mortgage payment, MP*

$$MP = \left[\frac{B(r_e)}{1 - \dfrac{1}{(1 + r_e)^n}} \right]$$

Where B is the amount borrowed or original loan balance, r_e is the effective monthly rate (annual rate/12) and n is the number of months for the loan (number of years x 12).

11. *Loan Amortization*

Loan interest = Beginning of month balance x effective monthly rate

Scheduled principal payment = Mortgage payment – Loan Interest

End of month balance = Beginning of month balance – Scheduled principal repayment

12. *Yield Spreads*

Yield spread = Yield on bond A – Yield on bond B

Relative yield spread = (Yield on bond A – Yield on bond B)/ (Yield on bond B)

Yield ratio = Yield on bond A / Yield on bond B

Bond B, the reference bond is normally an on-the-run treasury security.

13. After tax yield

After-tax yield = Pre-tax yield x (1 – Marginal tax rate)

14. Taxable-equivalent yield

Taxable equivalent yield = Tax-exempt yield/ (1-Marginal tax rate)

15. Valuing a bond

Value of a bond is the sum of the present values of the cash flows from the bond (like any other asset) or

$$V = PV_1 + PV_2 + \ldots + PV_n$$

Each present value is given by $PV_t = CF_t / (1+r)^t$ for annual cash flows or $PV_n = CF_n / [1+(r/2)]^n$ for semi-annual cash flows where r is the annual discount rate, t is the time and n is the number of periods (for annual cash flows, n = t and for semi-annual, n=2t). Valuation also done with different discount rates for each cash flow based on a term structure of interest rates.

16. Valuing a zero-coupon bond

$$V = \frac{FV}{\left(1+\frac{r}{2}\right)^{2n}}$$

Where FV is the face value of the bond and is received on maturity, r is the annual discount rate, and n is the number of years. This is in line with semi-annual payments approach for coupon bonds.

17. Finding the Full Price (or dirty price), V_F of a bond between coupon payments

$$V_F = \sum_{t=1}^{n} \frac{CF_t}{\left[1+\left(r/2\right)\right]^{t-1+w}}$$

Where r is the annual discount rate, CF_t is the semi-annual cash flow in period t, and n is the number of periods of cashflows remaining. w is the fractional period between settlement date and next coupon as is given by:

w = (Days between settlement date and next coupon payment) / (Days between coupon payments)

When w=1, we have the pricing of a bond on coupon dates.

18. Accrued interest, AI

AI = Semiannual coupon payment * (1-w)

Where w is as earlier defined and (1-w) is the fraction of the period of accrued interest days.

AI = (Semi annual coupon payment x Days in Accrued Interest period) / (Days in coupon period)

19. Clean Price of a Bond

Clean price = Full price – Accrued interest = V_F – AI

20. Current Yield

Current yield = Annual coupon payment / Bond Market Price

Other yield measures include the yield-to-maturity (YTM) of a bond which is the internal rate of return of the bond, or the yield that makes the present value of the cash flows equal to the bond market price. The Bond equivalent yield is double the semi-annual YTM.

21. *Bond equivalent yield of annual pay bond, BEY$_A$*

$BEY_A = 2\ [(1+\text{Yield on annual pay bond})^{0.5} -1]$

By making the Yield on annual pay bond the subject of the equation above with some algebraic manipulation, we obtain:

Yield on annual-pay bond $= [1+ (BEY_A/2)]^2 -1$

22. *Bond equivalent yield from monthly yields (MBS and ABS)*

Effective semiannual yield $= (1 + \text{Monthly yield})^6 -1$

Cash Flow yield $= 2 \times$ **Effective semiannual yield**

23. *Spread for Life (or simple margin) for a floater*

$$\text{Spread for life} = \left[\frac{100(100 - \text{Price})}{\text{Maturity}} + \text{Margin basis points}\right]\left(\frac{100}{\text{Price}}\right)$$

Where price is the price of the floater per $100 of par value, maturity is the term of the bond and margin basis points is the quoted margin in the coupon reset formula in basis points (note: 100 basis points = 1%)

24. *Yield on Treasury Bills, d*

$$d = (1-p)\left(\frac{360}{N_{SM}}\right)$$

Where d is the yield on a discount basis, p is the settlement price per $1 of face value and N_{SM} is the number of days between the settlement date and the maturity date. Given the yield on discount basis d

25. Interpolating between yields to find a yield, r_t

Interpolating between a lower maturity n year yield, r_n, and a higher maturity m year yield, r_m, is giving by the formula:

$$r_t = r_n + \left(\frac{r_m - r_n}{m-n} \right)(t-n)$$

Each yield can then be used for individual valuation of a cash flow to find a bond present value in a net present value methodology.

26. Zero-volatility spread or Z-Spread

The Z-spread is a spread, when added to the Treasury spot rates and used to discount the cashflows from a non-Treasury bond will give the market price of the non-Treasury security i.e. net present values of the cashflows discounted at the treasury spot rates plus the Z-spread gives the non-Treasury bond's price. It is obtained by trial-and-error.

Z-spread = OAS + Option cost   ;   Option cost = Z-spread - OAS

The OAS is the option adjusted spread, derived from a model dependent valuation for bonds with embedded options. The Z-spread is sometimes called the zero-volatility OAS, referring to interest rate volatility.

When there is little divergence between the nominal spread and the z-spread, the equation above can be written as:

Nominal spread ≈ OAS + Option cost

27. Forward rates

To calculate an n-period forward rate m periods from now, $_nf_m$, the following illustration is helpful.

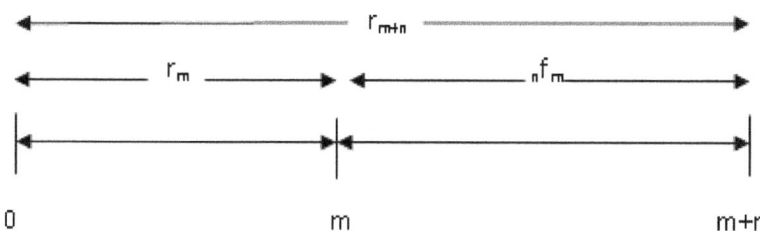

$$_nf_m = \left[\frac{(1+r_{m+n})^{m+n}}{(1+r_m)^m}\right]^{(1/n)} - 1$$

When n =1, the formula becomes a 1-period forward rate. This 1 period could be a year, six months or any other period. Care should be taken to adjust the rates accordingly from an annual rate to an effective rate per period e.g. if six monthly, annual rates divided by 2.

28. Relationship between spot rates, r_T, and forward rates, $_nf_m$

$$r_T = [(1+r_1)\,(1+_1f_1)\,(1+_1f_2)\,(1+_1f_3)\ldots\,(1+_1F_{T-1})]^{(1/T)} - 1$$

29. Convexity, C

$$C = \frac{V\,down + V\,up - 2V}{2(V)(\Delta y)^2}$$

30. Approximate percentage price change of a bond, (100*ΔP/P)

$$\frac{100\Delta P}{P} = 100\left[-D \times \Delta y + C \times (\Delta y)^2\right]$$

Where D is duration, C is convexity, P is the original bond price and Δy is the yield change for which the price change is required in decimal (e.g. 4% = 0.04). Both duration and convexity adjustments are necessary for large changes in yield, while duration only adjustment is enough for small changes in yield.

31. Macaulay Duration and Modified Duration

$$\text{Macaulay duration} = \frac{1}{k(1 + YTM/k)} \frac{\sum\limits_{t=1}^{n} t \times (PVCF_t)}{\text{Bond Price}}$$

$$\text{Modified duration} = \frac{\text{Macaulay duration}}{(1 + YTM/k)}$$

Where k is the number of payment periods per year (k=2 for semi-annual payments), n is the number of periods until maturity, YTM is the yield-to-maturity of the bond and $PVCF_t$ is the present value of bond cash flow in period t, discounted at the YTM.

32. The Price Value of a Basis Point (PVBP)

PVBP = Bond initial Price – Price if yield is changed by 0.01% (1 basis point)

7. DERIVATIVES AND ALTERNATIVE INVESTMENTS

Futures

1. Payoff from a Forward Rate Agreement (FRA)

$$\text{Payoff} = NP \left[\frac{(r - r_k)\left(\dfrac{\text{Days in underlying rate}}{360} \right)}{1 + r\left(\dfrac{\text{Days in underlying rate}}{360} \right)} \right]$$

Where NP is the notional principal on which the contract is based, r is the underlying rate at expiration and r_k is the forward contract rate. A forward contract has the notation mxn FRA where m is time to expiration (in months) of the contract and m-n is the underlying rate (in months, translated to days). For example, a 3x6 FRA expires in 3 months with underlying rate 90-day LIBOR.

2. International Monetary Market (IMM) index

IMM index = 100 – Rate

Where Rate is the discount yield or the rate quoted as a percent priced into T-bill futures contract.

3. Actual futures price

$1,000,000[1 – (Rate/100) (90/360)]

Where Rate is in percent and Rate/100 is in decimal and the $1,000,000 factor is because each contract is based in $1 million notional principal of Eurodollars or T-bills.

Options

4. Payoff of an interest rate Call Option

$$\text{Payoff} = \text{NP}\left[\text{Max}\left[0,\left(r-r_k\right)\right]\left(\frac{\text{Days in underlying rate}}{360}\right)\right]$$

Where NP is the notional principal, r is the underlying rate at expiration and r_k is the exercise rate.

5. Payoff of an interest rate Put Option

$$\text{Payoff} = \text{NP}\left[\text{Max}\left[0,\left(r_k-r\right)\right]\left(\frac{\text{Days in underlying rate}}{360}\right)\right]$$

Where NP is the notional principal, r is the underlying rate at expiration and r_k is the exercise rate.

6. Payoff of a call option on expiration

$$\textbf{Payoff} = \textbf{Max}\ [0,\ (S_T - X)]$$

7. Payoff of a put option on expiration

$$\textbf{Payoff} = \textbf{Max}\ [0,\ (X - S_T)]$$

Where S_T is the underlying's price at expiration and X is the exercise price or strike price. American and European options are equivalent at expiration.

8. Maximum value of options

$$c_0 \leq S_0,\ C_0 \leq S_0 \qquad\qquad p_0 \leq X/\left(1+r\right)^T,\ P_0 \leq X$$

Where c_0 and C_0 are European and American call options, and p_0 and P_0 are European and American put options. The minimum value of all options is zero.

9. *Lower bounds of options*

$c_0 \geq \text{Max} [0, S_0 - X/(1+r)^T]$, $C_0 \geq \text{Max} [(0, S_0 - X/(1+r)^T]$

$p_0 \geq \text{Max} [(0, X/(1+r)^T - S_0)$, $P_0 \geq \text{Max} (0, X - S_0)$

$C_o \geq c_o$ and $P_o \geq p_o$ which states that American options are always more valuable or have the same value as European options. Specifically, with no cash flows from underlying, $C_o = c_o$ and $C_o > c_o$ sometimes depending on cash flow magnitude. In most cases, $P_o > p_o$, especially with very low underlying price.

10. *Call and Put option prices as a result of different exercise prices*

$c_0 (X_1) \geq c_0 (X_2)$, $C_0 (X_1) \geq C_0 (X_2)$

$p_0 (X_2) \geq p_0 (X_1)$, $P_0 (X_2) \geq P_0 (X_1)$

Where X_2 is a higher exercise price than X_1

11. *Call and Put option prices as a result of different times to expiration*

$c_0 (T_2) \geq c_0 (T_1)$, $C_0 (T_2) \geq C_0 (T_1)$

$p_0 (T_2) \geq \text{or} \leq p_0 (T_1)$, $P_0 (T_2) \geq P_0 (T_1)$

Where T_2 is a longer time to expiration than T_1

12. *Put-Call Parity*

$S_0 + p_0 = c_0 + [X/(1+r)^T]$

This is a very important no-arbitrage condition for options and the put-call parity equation can be manipulated to derive synthetic securities by making one of the four components the subject of the formula. E.g. synthetic put, $p_0 = c_0 + [X/(1+r)^T] - S_0$. The combination of stock and put on the left side of the equation above is a protective put, while the equivalent right side is a fiduciary call.

13. Put-Call Parity with underlying paying dividends

$$S_0 - PV \text{ (cash flows from underlying)} + p_0 = c_0 + [X/(1+r)^T]$$

14. Lower bounds of options with cash flows from underlying

$$c_0 \geq \text{Max} [0, \{S_0 - PV \text{ (cash flows from underlying)}\} - (X/(1+r)^T)]$$

$$p_0 \geq \text{Max} [0, (X/(1+r)^T) - \{S_0 - PV \text{ (cash flows from underlying)}\}]$$

15. Profit at expiration, Π, from option positions

Long call: $\Pi = c_T - c_0$ where c_T is max $(0, S_T - X)$

Long put: $\Pi = p_T - p_0$ where p_T is max $(0, X - S_T)$

Covered call: $\Pi = (S_T - S_O) + (c_0 - c_T)$ where c_T is max $(0, S_T - X)$

Protective put: $\Pi = (S_T - S_O) + (p_T - p_0)$ where p_T is max $(0, X - S_T)$

The maximum payoff from a long call position is ∞ and from a long put position is X. The maximum loss for each long position is c_0 for a call and p_0 for a put. Bear in mind the payoffs (or profits) for a short position is that of the long position multiplied by -1 (zero sum instruments). The covered call is a long position in a stock and a short position in the call. The protective put is a long position in the stock and a long position in the put.

Swaps

16. Swap payment

Swap payment = Notional Principal x Swap rate x (Days in period/Days in year)

This also applies to currency swaps where the Notional principal is in the appropriate currency. Days in year could be 360 or 365 day conventions. The swap rate is in decimals in the equation above and could be a fixed rate for a fixed rate payment or floating rate for a floating rate payment.

17. Equity swap payment

Equity swap payment = Notional Principal x [(final Index level/initial index level)-1]

Alternative Investments

18. Income approach to real estate valuation

Appraisal price = Net Operating Income/ Market Capitalization rate

Market capitalization rate = Benchmark Net Operating Income/ Benchmark transaction price

This page is left intentionally blank

www.ingramcontent.com/pod-product-compliance
Lightning Source LLC
Chambersburg PA
CBHW081552170526
45166CB00009B/2673